"Team God"

Daily Devotionals

By

Michelle McCaleb

An Invitation

I want to personally invite you to be on God's team.
Being on God's team will allow you to always be on
the winning team.

Unlike other teams that never know the outcome,
God's team always wins. Join God's team. You may
think to yourself, "How do I get on God's team?" The
answer is to say, "I'm in!" Let God know that you
choose him. God always has a place for you on his
team. Not only does God want you on his team, but
he wants you to bring others to his team as well.

The choice is yours. God allows us to choose the team
that we want to be on. If you think that you are not
worthy, think again. God wants all of us on his team,
regardless of our sins, regardless of our past
relationships, regardless of where we are at today.
We can't handle the problems of life by ourselves, but
with God we can overcome anything. The choice is
ours.

Choose love, choose joy, choose peace, choose kindness, and choose Team God!

Dedication

I want to dedicate this book to my family. Family is one of God's many blessings. I cherish all of my family and thank God daily for each family member.

It is my hope and prayer that this book will land in the hands of people all across the world to bring them to God. I have much faith that God will make that happen.

We all face challenges in our lives, but through God, all things are possible!

We all face difficult times. God did not promise everyday would be perfect, but what he did promise was never to leave us. If you have difficult times, family issues, financial issues, stress, work problems, or perhaps addictions, then give it to God. God is waiting patiently for you.

To you, the reader, I pray for God to fill you with Godly wisdom for understanding what is truly important. Through God, you can be blessed with a future of eternal life with Jesus Christ.

Also, I pray that just as God has blessed me, he will bring blessings to you through this book.

May you always follow God's path to receive God's blessings!

Attribute

Psalm 25:12-13 (TLB)

12 Where is the man who fears the Lord? God will teach him how to choose the best. **13** He shall live within God's circle of blessing, and his children shall inherit the earth.

We all have something to offer to others. If you look around, you will be able to find at least one thing that you have that you can offer to others.

If we take the focus off ourselves and begin to focus on others then we can truly begin to realize we do have something to offer.

It may be a listening ear, a shoulder to cry on, a place to let someone get out of the cold, or a hot meal. It is amazing what conversations about God can come from sharing a batch of cookies.

God made each one of us with special attributes. He designed each one of us unique. We can all become leaders for God even if you have just begun to lead a life of God.

If you fear the Lord, have love for others, and you're willing to give of yourself, then you too can be a leader for God. What attributes do you have?

Offering

1 Timothy 4:14-15 (NKJV)

[14] Do not neglect the gift that is in you, which was given to you by prophecy with the laying on of the hands of the eldership. [15] Meditate on these things; give yourself entirely to them, that your progress may be evident to all.

Do you give to God? Do you give your first of everything to God? When God gives you an income, do you thank him for that and give back?

Do you give your time to God? Do you talk to God in prayer? Do you thank him for all that he has given you?

Do you give of yourself? Do you help others in need? Do you give to the poor that are hungry? Do you help your neighbor that may be in need?

Do you talk to others about God? Do you invite others to church?

With each new day brings new opportunities; Opportunities to be a leader for God. Ask God to make you aware if there is someone that does not know him. Ask God to give you the words to tell others about him.

Detail

Jeremiah 29:11 (NKJV)

[11] For I know the thoughts that I think toward you, says the Lord, thoughts of peace and not of evil, to give you a future and a hope.

Do you pay attention to details? Do you follow instructions?

When you're faced with challenges, do you listen to the voice inside of you that tells you to do the right thing?

Do you take the easy road when the choice arises? Do you take the road less traveled so that you will be sure to make the right choice?

Listen to the voice inside of you telling you to make that good choice. Listen to God.

God knows the plans that he has set for you and to do God's will requires us to pay attention to detail.

Take the opportunity to always make the right choice. Even when no one else knows your choices, God does.

Follower of Christ

1 John 4:20 (NKJV)

20 If someone says, "I love God," and hates his brother, he is a liar; for he who does not love his brother whom he has seen, how can he love God whom he has not seen?

Do you say that you love God, but you hate your brother?

Do you say that you love God but you can't forgive a friend for a sin against you?

What is important to God should also be important to you.

What's important to God is that we love like he does. That means that we are to love those that hurt or ridicule us. We are to love our brothers and sisters. We are to love our church family. We are to forgive everyone that hurts us.

That's what is important to God.

We are to love imperfect people because we are not perfect and God loves us anyways.

Obstacles

James 1:6 (NKJV)

[6] But let him ask in faith, with no doubting, for he who doubts is like a wave of the sea driven and tossed by the wind.

What obstacles are you facing? What is keeping you from God?

With God in your life, you can be sure that any obstacles can be destroyed.

Do you have obstacles that keep you from doing the things that you know you should be doing?

Ask yourself this one simple question, "Do I feel God's presence?"

If the answer is no then you have obstacles. Focus on all the things that keep you from God. Once you realize the things that are keeping you from God then you can begin to ask God to move those obstacles for you.

Once you begin asking God, he will have the opportunity to help you. God will not push himself on you but once invited he can begin moving the greatest of obstacles in your life.

No obstacle is too big for God. It's not the tears or the pain that will have the biggest impact, it's the faith that you have in God that he cherishes.

*It pleases God
when we serve
as a link to him.*

Are you linked to God?

Sacrifices

Hebrews 13:16 (NKJV)

16 But do not forget to do good and to share, for with such sacrifices God is well pleased.

In the Bible there are many stories about sacrifices. What a sacrifice that God made for us!

What sacrifices do we make? Do you ever give up anything?

What most people don't realize is that we must give in order to receive.

If we are going to live our lives like God it will require "Giving."

Ask yourself, "How much do I really give of myself?" In one single day, if you search hard enough, you can find at least one person in need. Choose to give of yourself.

Take the time to find that one family member that is lost. When we die we don't want one of our family members to not make it to Heaven. Begin giving of yourself. Take the time to encourage and invite that person to church.

Take the time to help your neighbor that may be in need. Just as God sacrificed his Son for our sins, sacrifice your needs and time to tend to others. For when we give, (we may not realize at the time) we will receive in return for the sacrifices that we make.

Right Words

James 1:18 (NKJV)

¹⁸ Of His own will He brought us forth by the word of truth, that we might be a kind of firstfruits of His creatures.

How many times have you said something that you wished that you could take back?

What we say is one of the most difficult things that people deal with. Talking bad about others, gossiping, and slander, can be a very bad habit for most.

Recognizing just how harmful our words can be is a start. Ask God to help you in this area. If others are gossiping, choose to remove yourself from the conversation or have the courage to let others know that their words are damaging.

Before you know it, with God's help you can begin to pay attention to the things that you say, and those harsh words can begin to stop.

Saying kind words, encouraging others, and making others feel good about themselves is very pleasing to God.

Ask God to help you say only the "Right words!"

Destined for Greatness

Genesis 12:2-3 (NKJV)

[2] I will make you a great nation; I will bless you and make your name great; and you shall be a blessing. [3] I will bless those who bless you, and I will curse him who curses you; and in you all the families of the earth shall be blessed."

Have you ever noticed that some families just seem to have it all? They may have a nice home, lots of money, nice cars, and their children may go to the finest schools, and they all end up with good careers that provide an excellent income.

Even successful people have challenges and obstacles.

With successful people, you will find a family that prays together, that prays for their children daily, and that leads their children to God.

Even successful Godly people will struggle at times but their struggles are easier since God is in control.

Your family can be successful too if you allow God to lead you. Godly wisdom is the key to success.

You may ask, "How can I turn my struggles into success?" There is one sure way, and that's with God leading you every step of the way.

Begin with prayer and you too can be destined for greatness!

Relationships

1 Corinthians 15:33 (NKJV)

[33] Do not be deceived: "Evil company corrupts good habits." [34] Awake to righteousness, and do not sin; for some do not have the knowledge of God…

Do you continuously hang out with people that show no signs of God? Do you surround yourself with people that make Godly decisions?

We can very easily get off of God's path if we allow the wrong people into our lives. Satan will throw curve balls at us every chance that he can. Keep your guard up at all times to shield your heart from bad influences.

Pray for God to send you Christian friends and shield you from evil-doers so you will not get drawn into their sins.

Deciding to hang out with the right people can be one of the most important decisions we make. Pray for discernment to know which friends are the right friends.

It pleases God
when we serve
as a link to him.

Are you linked to God?

Missed Opportunities

Matthew 6:1-4 (NKJV)

[1] "Take heed that you do not do your charitable deeds before men, to be seen by them. Otherwise you have no reward from your Father in heaven. [2] Therefore, when you do a charitable deed, do not sound a trumpet before you as the hypocrites do in the synagogues and in the streets, that they may have glory from men. Assuredly, I say to you, they have their reward. [3] But when you do a charitable deed, do not let your left hand know what your right hand is doing, [4] that your charitable deed may be in secret; and your Father who sees in secret will Himself reward you openly.

How many times have you passed up an opportunity to do something that you wished you would have done?

How many times have you gone to church and never took the opportunity to invite one of your family members?

How many times have you gone out to lunch and a co-worker couldn't go because they didn't have the money? Do you wish that just one time you would have included that co-worker?

Do we really take the time to listen to others when they tell us about a need they have?

Life is full of missed opportunities. The difference between an opportunity and a missed opportunity is not a lack of ability but a lack of desire.

Do you desire to help others? Do you desire to give of your time? Do you give of yourself without seeking recognition?

If you take the opportunity to give to those that are hurting, before you know it your heart will be so full of love and joy that the hurting you experience will begin to dissolve.

Do a good deed without seeking anything in return. When no one else knows, God does!

Testimony

Matthew 5:16 (NKJV)

[16] Let your light so shine before men, that they may see your good works and glorify your Father in heaven.

Do you have a testimony that you can share with others?

When others see the things that you are doing, can they see a true testimony in you? Can they see a living, breathing testimony?

If you're not living your life in the way others see a testimony, then it's not too late to begin living a life full of God.

It's all in the choices that you make. Ask yourself, "Do I want to turn my life around and begin to receive the blessings that God has for me?"

Once you make the decision to follow God, you too will have a testimony about your relationship with God.

Others will begin to see the changes in you. When you share your testimony with others, you are doing God's work.

God wants us to bring others to him. This life on earth is temporary, living eternity in Heaven will be forever!

Inheritance

Exodus 34:7 (NKJV)

[7] keeping mercy for thousands, forgiving iniquity and transgression and sin, by no means clearing *the guilty,* visiting the iniquity of the fathers upon the children and the children's children to the third and the fourth generation."

Have you ever received an inheritance?

Do you plan ahead so you can leave your children an inheritance?

You can save money your entire life to leave your children an inheritance, but truly there is no inheritance that is equal to or greater than a spiritual inheritance to leave your children.

If you lead a life that is pleasing to God, he will bless your children, your children's children, and generations to follow.

Teach your children the ways of the Lord so they will not depart from him.

If you teach your children, and lead a Godly life, you can begin to receive all of God's inheritance in your life here on earth, as well as, the inheritance of entering God's Kingdom.

Give your family the greatest inheritance ever, teach them about God and let them reap the benefits.

There is no greater inheritance than to receive God's inheritance!

Step Up!

Jeremiah 33:3 (AMP)

[3] Call to Me and I will answer you and show you great and mighty things, fenced in *and* hidden, which you do not know (do not distinguish and recognize, have knowledge of and understand).

Have you ever played ball and it's your time to step up to the plate to bat? If so, you know that can bring some anxiety or excitement.

Have you ever had to speak publicly in front of people and got anxiety?

Stepping up can come from lots of events or activities, but the step up that I'm referring to is stepping up to do God's work.

Stepping up may bring anxiety because it may require letting go of your old way of doing things.

Stepping up may mean changing friends, activities, bad habits, and the list goes on and on.

Step up so you can begin to have a better way of living!

It pleases God
when we serve
as a link to him.

Are you linked to God?

Great Story

Philippians 1:22-23 (TLB)

²² But if living will give me more opportunities to win people to Christ, then I really don't know which is better, to live or die! ²³ Sometimes I want to live, and at other times I don't, for I long to go and be with Christ. How much happier for *me* than being here!

Isn't it great when we turn on the news and can actually hear a great story?

Usually the news is full of horrific crimes, and stories of bad things.

When others see you, what kind of story do they read?

Do you have a story that is good or bad? If your story is bad, it's not too late to turn your life into a story that is awesome to read.

Start with the first chapter of your new book. Let God lead you into a new life story that will be remarkable.

You may ask, "How can I begin?" The best way to start is in the word of God. If you're not accustomed to reading, then just begin with one page at a time. That's how your new story can begin, one day at a time!

Storms

Matthew 24:13 (TLB)

[13] But those enduring to the end shall be saved.

Do you take cover when a storm is coming? Do you make preparations for that storm? Does your family seek the safest place to go?

There will be many storms in life. We never know when those storms will come. Meteorologists will predict the storms.

God is the only one that knows when the storms will arrive, how long they will stay and who they will affect.

If we seek God for refuge, not only in the storms, we can take comfort in knowing that we will be safe.

If God resides in you, if he is with you during all the storms in life, you will be able to experience the, 'calm' before, during, and after the storms of life.

Vessel

Acts 3:6 (TLB)

[6] But Peter said, "We don't have any money for you! But I'll give you something else! I command you in the name of Jesus Christ of Nazareth, *walk!"*

Does God work through you? Do you allow yourself to be led by God?

If you will allow God to lead you, you can be led to places that are awesome.

On any given day think of your routine. Is your routine full of helping others? Is your routine only of yourself?

Allow God to bless others through you. Just as God has blessed you, share those blessings with others.

How can you begin? Start with charities. There are many people that God uses as a vessel to help others. Search for the organization in your community that is designed to help those that are less fortunate. Donate your time to help. Once you begin helping, many doors will open for you. Opening the right doors to get to God will lead you to the best destination _EVER_!

Steps

Psalm 37:23 (TLB)

[23] The steps of good men are directed by the Lord. He delights in each step they take.

When you walk daily, do you realize just how important your steps are?

Do you realize how important the role each part of your body has?

Your feet have the job of carrying your body. Your hand has a major role in the things that you're asked to do.

Your heart has an important role because without your heart working properly, you would not be able to survive.

Do you understand just how important the right steps in your life can be? If you take the wrong steps, it can lead to a life of destruction.

If you follow God's footsteps, you will be able to realize just how important the right steps are.

With a God-filled life, your heart will be full with many blessings of joy!

Always ask God to lead your steps!

It pleases God
when we serve
as a link to him.

Are you linked to God?

Purpose

Proverbs 2:1-5 (TLB)

2 ¹⁻² Every young man who listens to me and obeys my instructions will be given wisdom and good sense. ³⁻⁵ Yes, if you want better insight and discernment, and are searching for them as you would for lost money or hidden treasure, then wisdom will be given you and knowledge of God himself; you will soon learn the importance of reverence for the Lord and of trusting him.

Do you have a purpose? Is there a reason behind all the decisions that you make? We must all have a purpose. Without a purpose we will be without direction.

Ask God to reveal to you what your purpose is. God has plans for each of us, but until we take the time to listen to God, we will not fully understand exactly what he has planned for us.

When we focus on God and doing his work, we will be sure to find our purpose.

When we focus on God it is truly amazing how suddenly our vision can be restored. What I am referring to is our ability to see what is important to God. Things that we put our value in suddenly become less important.

God has a plan for every single one of us. Seek God to find your purpose.

Directions

Matthew 19:17 (TLB)

"…But to answer your question, you can get to heaven if you keep the commandments."

When you are traveling to a place that you've never been, do you know how to follow directions?

When you are given an assignment, do you follow the instructions?

When you're putting something together, do you follow the instructions so you will end up with a completed project?

What about God's instructions? Do you follow those instructions daily? He gave us commandments to live by. Do you live your life according to the commandments? Do you focus on the written instructions that God gave to each of us?

Following instructions are very important, especially when they come from God.

By following his instructions you can be sure to land in the direction that God intended for us.

Letting Go

2 Chronicles 7:14 (TLB)

then **if my people** will humble themselves and pray, and search for me, and turn from their wicked ways, I will hear them from heaven and forgive their sins and heal their land.

What are you holding on to from the past that is keeping you from moving forward?

Do you always remember a past sin that you committed? Does that sin weigh you down?

Do you hold on to unforgiveness where someone has hurt you?

Do you hold on to bitterness where something didn't go your way?

What are you holding on to that you need to let go of?

Let it go! Let go of the sin, forgive yourself and ask God to forgive you for the sins you have committed against him.

Let it go! Let go of the unforgiveness and bitterness so you can move forward without these things weighing you down.

Instead, hold on to God and everything good, so you can move forward and live a rewarding life free of your past mistakes. Let it go!

Guard Your Heart

2 Samuel 22:31 (TLB)

[31] As for God, his way is perfect; the word of the Lord is true. He shields all who hide behind him.

Our heart is vital to the functioning of our body. Our heart has a very important role. We should be guarding our hearts from anything that could damage it.

Are you doing anything to damage your heart? Are you smoking cigarettes? Are you allowing evil to touch your heart? Are you filtering out bad things?

We should all guard our hearts from anything that is not of God. Ask yourself when doing things that you're not sure of if it's good or bad. Ask if God would be pleased. If God is not in your choices, then shield yourself from making those bad choices.

Fill your heart with good so you will have no room for the bad in your heart.

It pleases God when we serve as a link to him.

Are you linked to God?

One in Christ

1 Peter 1:14-16 (TLB)

¹⁴ Obey God because you are his children; don't slip back into your old ways—doing evil because you knew no better. ¹⁵ But be holy now in everything you do, just as the Lord is holy, who invited you to be his child. ¹⁶ He himself has said, "You must be holy, for I am holy."

Do you put on your best clothes, best attitude, best everything when you go to church and then when you leave church you show no signs of God?

We should all bring our glory to God when we go to his holy place and we should always give God our best every single day.

How often do you pray? Do you only go to God in prayer when you need something?

How often are you thanking God for all your blessings?

Have you ever read the best seller called "The Bible?"

You may think you know God's word, but until you get into the word of God, can you truly know what God's word is all about?

When you open your Bible, you are opening a whole new beginning, a beginning that will lead to a wonderful ending, eternity with God and all the people that know and love God.

What a blessing to be one in Christ!

Struggles

Mark 4:12 (TLB)

11-12 He replied, "You are permitted to know some truths about the Kingdom of God that are hidden to those outside the Kingdom: 'Though they see and hear, they will not understand or turn to God, or be forgiven for their sins.'

What do you struggle with? Do you struggle with fear? Do you struggle with lack of patience? Do you struggle with addictions, finances, or loneliness?

Whatever you struggle with, ask yourself, "Is God in this?" If you have not allowed God to help you with all of your struggles, then today can be a new beginning for you.

How do you begin? Start with prayer. Start by asking God to help you with all your struggles. Prayer will begin the communication and allow God to take care of your needs. God has been waiting patiently on all of us. God is patient, and has no fears. God can deliver you from any addiction, or financial problem. When you're done, always remember, God is with you. He will not leave you or forsake you.

Qualified

Matthew 9:37-38 (TLB)

[37] "The harvest is so great, and the workers are so few," he told his disciples. [38] "So pray to the one in charge of the harvesting, and ask him to recruit more workers for his harvest fields."

Are you a leader for God? What makes us qualified? Are you actively involved in doing God's work? Do you help others in need? Do you step up and teach others about God? What makes us qualified?

God made us qualified when he paid the price for our sins on the cross. God made each of us. He designed us unique in our special way. God wants us to be leaders for him. He wants us to teach others about his word.

It pleases God when we help a stranger in need. By doing just that you are being a leader for God, when you help a family member that is having a difficult time, that's being a leader for God.

By doing good, by helping others, you are setting examples for others. Let others see God through you! Yes, we are qualified!

Shaken

Isaiah 48:17 (TLB)

¹⁷ The Lord, your Redeemer, the Holy One of Israel, says: I am the Lord your God, who punishes you for your own good and leads you along the paths that you should follow.

Do you ever get shaken up? Do you find yourself facing struggles that just seemed to pop out unexpectedly?

We must constantly focus on God because we never know when Satan will try his best to attack us. By realizing that through life's struggles, and unexpected hardships that God is right there with us, we will be less shaken. We must trust in God in every single situation that he has a reason for allowing those shake ups to happen.

One really good lesson about any situation is what we learn from it. If you are faced with shaky situations, and you made a bad choice that led you to that situation, then take the opportunity to talk to God about it. God sometimes allows us to get shaken just so we can get back on his path.

It pleases God
when we serve
as a link to him.

Are you linked to God?

Hard Times

1 Thessalonians 5:16 (TLB)

[16] Always be joyful. [17] Always keep on praying. [18] No matter what happens, always be thankful, for this is God's will for you who belong to Christ Jesus.

It is easy to praise God when things are good. It is easier to give God all the credit for our blessings when everything is going as planned.

But what about the days that are not so good? When times are hard, when your family is suffering, and when everything seems to be falling apart? Do you praise God during those times?

When it's hardest to pray, pray harder! When you think that you don't have anything to be thankful for, thank God even more!

Don't let the devil steal your joy. Turn only to God, turn away from your sin and praise God for he is the one that gives those blessings.

Wake Up Call

John 5:8 (NLT)

[8] Jesus told him, "Stand up, pick up your mat, and walk!"

Do you have a hard time waking up each morning as you should? Do you need an alarm clock?

When God gives you a wakeup call, do you notice? When you think that all is lost or unfixable, do you realize that God is giving you that wakeup call?

Wake up, look around, God is all around you. He can be within you if you just adhere to the wakeup call.

God's calling, you just have to listen and answer the call.

When you think all is lost, think again. God waits patiently and doesn't want anyone left asleep.

Help

James 4:10 (NLT)

¹⁰ Humble yourselves before the Lord, and he will lift you up in honor.

When you need help, who do you turn to? When you are traveling and not sure if you're going in the right direction, do you stop to ask for directions?

Are you scared to ask for help? Do you feel as though you will be belittled if you ask for help? Do you feel like you're above asking?

It is amazing what asking for help can do for our outcomes. When we humble ourselves to admit that we need help, at any age, God will help the humble.

When you ask God for help, he will draw close to you. Give yourself humbly to God and resist the devil and he will flee from you.

Realizing you need help is a great beginning. Asking for help will give you a great ending.

We all need help, even when we don't realize it.

Anointed

1 John 2:27 (NLT)

²⁷ But you have received the Holy Spirit, and he lives within you, so you don't need anyone to teach you what is true. For the Spirit teaches you everything you need to know, and what he teaches is true—it is not a lie. So just as he has taught you, remain in fellowship with Christ.

Many years ago, anoint came from putting oil on a sheep's heads to protect them from insects. Today many people use an anointing oil to signify a blessing on others. The oil itself is not to be used as a magic potion, but rather it's to be a symbol of what God is doing.

God has anointed all Christians for a specific purpose. Do you know what your purpose is? Has God revealed to you what he wants you to do? Have you taken the time to listen to God?

When you hear the voice in you telling you something good that needs to be done, do you take the time to do that good deed?

When you hear the voice telling you to do something that may be out of your comfort zone, do you listen?

Sometimes doing God's work may be challenging, but God has chosen us to do his work. Are you allowing God to use you to get his work done?

It pleases God
when we serve
as a link to him.

Are you linked
to God?

Freedom

John 8:36 (NLT)

[36] So if the Son sets you free, you are truly free.

So many people don't fully understand just how great it is to have freedom. God paid the ultimate sacrifice for us to have freedom. He freed us from our sin. One man, one amazing man did that for everyone.

We have a choice every day of our lives when we awake. We can choose to carry around sin or we can choose to have freedom.

When we make mistakes, we must confess those sins and ask for forgiveness. By doing that, we can release the weight that we have been carrying around of those sins. By confessing, we can experience freedom.

Freedom from sins keeps Satan away. When you live a life full of God, Satan flees from you. Satan can't stand against God. It's an impossible task for the devil.

Repenting of your sins and living a Godly life brings the freedom that will keep us living in the fullness of God on earth and an eternal life in heaven <u>forever</u>.

Challenges

Proverbs 3:6 (NLT)

[6] Seek his will in all you do, and he will show you which path to take.

What challenges do you face? Do you face difficult times? Is the road you're on constantly a dirt road?

You may be asking yourself, "How can I get on the paved road?" You can get on the right road by following God.

Were you in the habit of thinking God was supposed to be following you? Are your conversations with God all about telling him what you need, and asking, asking, and more asking?

If so, here is how you can begin to get off the dirt road. Begin by being thankful. Tell God just how thankful you are for all that he has done for you. Begin to communicate with God, not only when you think you need something. By having a thankful heart, you will please God. God will then help with those challenges that you're facing.

Pray Hard

Philippians 4:6 (NLT)

[6] Don't worry about anything; instead, pray about everything. Tell God what you need, and thank him for all he has done.

Do you have a hard time praying when times are hard? If so, you should pray hard even when it is the hardest to pray.

Communicating with God through prayer is the very first step in your relationship with the Lord.

God knows every single thing that we need, he loves to hear that we need him and want him with us at all times.

Pray hard, beginning with "thanks." Even when we feel that we don't have anything to be thankful for, we do. If you look around, you can find things that are a blessing. Thank God for the things that you do have instead of focusing on more.

So many people live today being self-centered instead of being God-centered.

God can provide for us everything that we need, but we have to pray for it. When we pray to God our heart opens up for so much more.

Prayer will keep the right doors opening in our lives, but without prayer, all the wrong doors will be open.

Pray hard when you find it too hard to pray.

Love Your Church

1 Corinthians 12:22-23 (NLT)

22 In fact, some parts of the body that seem weakest and least important are actually the most necessary. 23 And the parts we regard as less honorable are those we clothe with the greatest care. So we carefully protect those parts that should not be seen,

If you want to build a strong foundation in your church, you must commit yourself to it. You must stand alongside, despite all its faults, you must meet the needs necessary for growth and you must cherish it by protecting and guarding it.

How many times do we walk away from a church because someone makes us mad or hurts our feelings? Satan works hard to get to people that know God because he already has a hold of the people that don't know him.

Going to church can be easy, but staying can be hard. Because everything is not always perfect.

If we love like God does, then we can be certain to stay in church. Choose to love others, even when they hurt you. It's not okay to walk away just because you get offended. God wants us to stick it out. People will let you down even when they don't mean to.

One thing is for certain; God will never leave you nor forsake you.

It pleases God
when we serve
as a link to him.

Are you linked
to God?

Destination

Deuteronomy 4:29 (NLT)

29 But from there you will search again for the Lord your God. And if you search for him with all your heart and soul, you will find him.

Do you know where you're going? Sometimes we all get distracted or simply lost.

Are you so focused on where you have been that you don't pay attention to where you're going?

Without the Bible, we have no directions. Without the presence of God, we simply get lost.

God says over and over again in the Bible that if we seek him, we will find him.

God doesn't hide from us. He wants us to find him. He wants us to always focus on our final destination.

If you're lost and can't seem to move forward, then seek God. God can help you move forward. In order to lead others to God, we must also lead people based on God's word, not ours. By doing great things, you're preparing for your future. If you're not sure what to do in your life, search for God. God's word will guide you to your destination.

Cherish

1 John 3:18 (NLT)

18 Dear children, let's not merely say that we love each other; let us show the truth by our actions.

What is important to you? What do you cherish the most? What lies within your heart?

If we focus on where we spend our time and money, we can begin to see just what we cherish the most.

Are you living your life focused on earthly possessions? Earthly possessions will come and go. Do you focus on where you will spend eternity?

If you have not lived your life focusing on God, then it's not too late.

Seek deep within your heart. Start by asking yourself what you really cherish. Is what you cherish pleasing to God?

If you haven't been cherishing the things that you should, ask God to help you to see what is truly important.

Asset

Romans 9:10 (NLT)

¹⁰ For it is by believing in your heart that you are made right with God, and it is by confessing with your mouth that you are saved.

Do you allow yourself to be an asset to God? Do you help God to share his word?

If you have not been in the habit of telling others about God, it's not too late to begin.

God is always with us. Sometimes we tend to walk away from God, so far even, that we don't listen when he is trying to get our attention.

We get so busy with our daily routines that sometimes we need to all slow down and listen to God.

If we wake up each morning and simply ask God to help us bring others to his word, then God will help.

We can be an asset to God, or we can choose not to be. Are you an asset?

Stumble

James 3:2 (NLT)

[2] Indeed, we all make many mistakes. For if we could control our tongues, we would be perfect and could also control ourselves in every other way.

When babies begin to walk, they stumble. It's the same with Christians in their walk with God.

Some days we may walk perfectly with God and other days we may feel like a baby learning how to walk.

We will all stumble from time to time because we are not perfect. When we make mistakes, the key to overcoming those mistakes is to admit to God that we have sinned. The next essential step is to ask God for forgiveness.

We all make the mistake of trying to justify our sins, however, sin is wrong. We all have to answer for the choices that we make.

While traveling on God's path, keep your eyes on God and your walk will be easier. Stumbling will happen from time to time, but less when you're focused on God!

It pleases God when we serve as a link to him.

Are you linked
to God?

Burden

Psalm 55:22 (NLT)

[22] Give your burdens to the Lord, and he will take care of you. He will not permit the godly to slip and fall.

Are you in the habit of looking at things as though they are a burden?

Do you spend your life being a burden to others?

If someone did an assessment of your life, would you be considered a burden or an asset?

The sin that we carry with us creates a huge burden. Before we know it, our sin has piled up.

In order to get rid of those burdens that we carry we must seek God. Not only must we seek God, but we must confess our sins. We must tell God we are sorry when we sin and also show God that we are sorry. If we show no signs of being sorry, then we will begin to take on all those bad habits that we have been accustomed to. Just like old things that we don't use any longer. We must get rid of our sins completely in order to get rid of our burdens.

Invitation

John 16:3 (NLT)

³ And this is the way to have eternal life—to know you, the only true God, and Jesus Christ, the one you sent to earth.

Isn't it nice to receive an invitation? An invitation makes us feel part of something. Maybe it's a graduation, a wedding shower, a birthday party, but whatever the occasion, we feel accepted.

Do you ever listen to God when he gives you an invitation? God wants to be in our lives every day.

Has anyone ever invited you to church? Don't wait on someone to invite you before you go. Listen to God's invitation, and let him lead you to a church that is right for you. God's invitation is for us to get into his word. Once we begin reading our Bible, God will become more and more real in our hearts. The Holy Spirit draws us and when he does, you will want to invite Jesus to come into your heart and he will accept our invitation to come into our hearts.

Invitations are awesome regardless if you're sending or receiving the invite.

Listen to God so you will not miss out on his invitation.

Link

Acts 10:35 (NLT)

[35] In every nation he accepts those who fear him and do what is right.

There are many links where we can go to find information that we are seeking. Links will take you to more and more information if you keep clicking on those links.

We can also be a link to God. We can give others information about God.

Are you a link for God? Do you encourage others to seek God? Do you invite others to come hear the word of God?

We should all be focusing on others to help as many people as we can. It pleases God when we serve as a link to him.

Do you take every opportunity to talk to others about God? If you don't know the words to say to encourage, then ask God to speak through you to others.

Be the link that will bring others to God!

Resolution

Psalm 105:3 (NLT)

[3] Exult in his holy name; rejoice, you who worship the Lord.

Sometimes things seem so impossible that we just can't seem to find a solution.

We all have problems, stress, and burdens that others aren't even aware of.

We may not always know how to handle the difficult times, but God knows. God knows what we feel every second of every day. He knows why we hurt and why we cry.

If you feel as though you're alone, think again. God will never leave us. If you have never communicated with God just start with prayer.

Alone we can't handle life's traumas, but with God we can handle anything. By believing in God, and having faith in him, your problems can be resolved.

Always remember God's timing is not our timing. Faith can bring resolution to those who seek God and trust in him.

It pleases God
when we serve
as a link to him.

Are you linked to God?

Perish

2 Peter 3:9 (NIV)

[9] The Lord is not slow in keeping his promise, as some understand slowness. Instead he is patient with you, not wanting anyone to perish, but everyone to come to repentance.

All things must come to an end at some point. Through God, our ending will be the beginning of eternity. Through God we will have an everlasting life that will never perish.

Material things of the world will come and go so do not set your sights on things of the world. Set your sight upon God.

If you focus on bringing others to God, then you will be doing work that is very pleasing to God. Set your sights on others so they too will have an everlasting life in Heaven.

Purity

Philippians 4:8 (NIV)

[8] Finally, brothers and sisters, whatever is true, whatever is noble, whatever is right, whatever is pure, whatever is lovely, whatever is admirable—if anything is excellent or praiseworthy—think about such things.

We all want the best things in life. When we go to the grocery store, we want the freshest bread. We want the best milk with the latest expiration date.

We want the best homes and cars for our families.

God wants the best for us too. God wants us to be pure. He wants us to be clean of sin. God wants us to live in a world that is pure. God doesn't like the world to be full of sin.

If you allow God in your heart, he can make you pure again. If you ask for forgiveness and allow God into your heart, he can wash away any uncleanliness in your life.

God is a forgiving God. He wants to make us pure. He died on the cross for our sins so we could be pure. Seek God in all that you do, and when you do make mistakes, give them to God to cleanse. God wants purity in our lives.

Respect

Colossians 3:25 (NIV)

[25] Anyone who does wrong will be repaid for their wrongs, and there is no favoritism.

Respect is something we all want. It is also something we have to give to others at times when we feel they may not be deserving of it.

Most times if we want respect we have to also be respectful of others.

How often do we respect the word of God? That should be the number one priority when giving respect.

God is our Creator. He made all things. The Bible clearly tells us how God made all things. Do you respect the things of God? If you're married, do you respect your marriage and treat that commitment as your most precious gift?

Are you one with God? Do you recognize God in your life and give him the greatest respect? We should all give God the respect and glory that he deserves. What God giveth, he can also take away. We should respect God with our mind and our mouth always. God wants us to tell others about him!

Obedient

Romans 2:8 (NIV)

[8] But for those who are self-seeking and who reject the truth and follow evil, there will be wrath and anger.

We all have rules that we must follow at some point in our lives. When we were children we had to obey our parents' rules. We had rules at school. If we played sports we had rules in the games.

Even as adults we still have rules to follow. Sometimes that can be a little trying, especially when we would rather do things our own way.

Most of the time our way doesn't work. When we try to live life the way we want, without guidance from God, we can go down a road that will lead to destruction.

Why do many people try to go by their own rules? Because it's easier to take the same road as everyone else. Stepping out to follow God's rules may seem harder. When, in fact, if we follow God's rules, our outcome will be eternity.

Disciplined

Hebrews 12:11 (NIV)

[11] No discipline seems pleasant at the time, but painful. Later on, however, it produces a harvest of righteousness and peace for those who have been trained by it.

To be successful in life we must be disciplined. To be a good parent requires discipline. Sometimes it's hard to discipline our children. Just knowing the outcome of teaching our children is the purpose driving the discipline.

To perfect a skill requires discipline. Have you ever known anyone that was successful that didn't have discipline?

If something is truly important to us then we must be disciplined. Too many people spend their time foolishly focusing on things which require no discipline at all.

Doing work for God requires discipline. How important is God in our life? Do we take the time to perfect things of God? Do we spend time daily doing what God wants us to do?

God expects us to be disciplined and be faithful to his laws. It clearly says in the Bible that God requires us to keep the commandments. Are we disciplined enough to keep the commandments that God requires?

Escape

Psalm 34:18 (NIV)

18 The Lord is   close to   the   brokenhearted and saves those who are crushed in spirit.

Do we ever feel the need to escape, to just get away from all the demands of life? Why do we all seem so busy? In today's society our schedules are maxed out. People don't seem to even have time to be still and focus on what's truly important.

Take a moment to focus on what is important to God. If we focus on what's important to God, then our overwhelming schedules can dwindle down.

If we all take the time to truly focus on God, and let him guide us, then we can begin to slow down.

We all need to escape from the demands of life so we can take time out to ask ourselves what we can let go of.

Doing God's work should come with excitement and joy.

Escaping from life's demands to find what God wants would be beneficial to us all.

Discernment

1 John 4:1 (NIV)

¹ Dear friends, do not believe every spirit, but test the spirits to see whether they are from God, because many false prophets have gone out into the world.

Life throws many challenges to each of us daily. If we don't watch out we can get caught up in things that we shouldn't be a part of.

Many people will come and go in our lives, but do we really choose the right people to hang out with?

Good friends can impact the choices that we make. How can we know which friends we should keep and which friends we should distance ourselves from? If we are unsure, ask God to help you with discernment to allow us to know which friends will bring us closer to God.

Many people will ask us to get involved with projects. It is easy to get involved with so much that we can't focus on what's truly important. We should always allow God to lead us in the projects that we get involved in. If God is leading us then we can't go wrong. By asking God to help us with discernment in every decision that we make, we will be sure to do God's work and accomplish the task.

Fruitful

Deuteronomy 4:9 (NIV)

[9] Only be careful, and watch yourselves closely so that you do not forget the things your eyes have seen or let them fade from your heart as long as you live. Teach them to your children and to their children after them.

Being fruitful is a gift from God. Do you ever notice people that are happy in all they do? Some people look at material things to determine if others are fruitful.

There are many people that are not happy no matter how much they have. They are always seeking more, such as a nicer home, or newer car, and the list can go on and on.

One thing is for sure, money can't buy happiness. By doing God's work and living a life that is pleasing to God, we can inherit things much more important than material things, such as peace, joy, and happiness.

When we are blessed with the fruits of the spirit, we can also pass that down to our children and their children so they can be fruitful. By teaching our children the way of the Lord, they can be blessed with many fruits.

Different

Deuteronomy 8:6 (NIV)

[6] Observe the commands of the Lord your God, walking in obedience to him and revering him.

Having God in our hearts changes everything. By choosing to live our lives following God, we will be different. It may seem hard at first to act differently, to speak differently, to have different friends and the list can go on and on.

It's okay to be different.

Once others begin to realize that we are Godly people, they will begin to notice good! God expects us to live our lives where others can see him. When others look at us, do they see God?

God is good. God is love. God is happiness. God is not having jealously in our lives. God is kind. God is forgiving. God wants us to help others. God loves everyone.

Do others see God when they look at us? Choose to be different than sinners. Choose to live your life full of God.

Character

1 Peter 1:15 (NIV)

[15] But just as he who called you is holy, so be holy in all you do;

Our actions and our character say a lot about us. How we handle stressful situations shows our character as well.

We may act one way when we don't have God in our lives, but with God we can be totally different.

With God we can overcome anything. You may be asking yourself, "How can I find God?" The best way to find God is through prayer and to read the word of God. God waits on each of us patiently to seek him.

With God in your life, a stressful situation can become less stressful. If we turn to God in every situation for guidance, he will lead you through it. Godly wisdom can help our character to change from bad to good.

God wants us to show good character to others. People always remember the way that you make them feel. Always treat others with the character of God. God wants us to be of good character.

ISBN-13:978-1497548459

ISBN-10:1497548454

www.three-sheep.com

Other Books Written by Author

If You are Praying, Why Worry? If You are Worrying, Pray by Michelle McCaleb

Other Books Written by Author's Grandson, Jaiden Gray

Turtle Boy by Jaiden Gray

About the Author

I am happily married to Jeff McCaleb and we have three children, Jamie, Lacey, and Evan. We reside in the middle of Tennessee and enjoy our two grandchildren, Jaidan and Paris, and we are actively involved in their lives as well.

In my daily life, I find that I cherish my 'God' time more and more. God has inspired me to write these daily devotionals. After spending alone time with God, he gives me the words to write to encourage another.

During the week, I spend my work days helping others with career guidance and counseling to help those who are disadvantaged or are facing challenges. I enjoy being a part of something that is so positive in the lives of others.

I enjoy attending church and have found that as life goes on, I want God to bless others as He has blessed me. Feeling God's presence comes with getting to know Him on a personal level and I find that reading the Bible daily helps my personal relationship with God.

Because I feel so strongly that knowing God on a personal level is the key, I have decided to write the daily devotionals in a book format to help others come to know God as I have.

Made in the USA
Columbia, SC
18 October 2022